Special Object Lessons
for Young Children

Object Lessons Series

Bess, C. W., *Children's Object Lessons from the Seasons,* 1026–8
Bess, C. W., *Object-Centered Children's Sermons,* 0734–8
Bess, C. W., *Sparkling Object Sermons for Children,* 0824–7
Bess, C. W., & Roy DeBrand, *Bible-Centered Object Sermons for Children,* 0886–7
Biller, Tom & Martie, *Simple Object Lessons for Children,* 0793–3
Bruinsma, Sheryl, *Easy-to-Use Object Lessons,* 0832–8
Bruinsma, Sheryl, *More Object Lessons for Very Young Children,* 1075–6
Bruinsma, Sheryl, *New Object Lessons,* 0775–5
Bruinsma, Sheryl, *Object Lessons for Every Occasion,* 0994–4
Bruinsma, Sheryl, *Object Lessons for Special Days,* 0920–0
Bruinsma, Sheryl, *Object Lessons for Very Young Children,* 0956–1
Claassen, David, *Object Lessons for a Year,* 2514–1
Connelly, H. W., *47 Object Lessons for Youth Programs,* 2314–9
Coombs, Robert, *Concise Object Sermons for Children,* 2541–9
Coombs, Robert, *Enlightening Object Lessons for Children,* 2567–2
Cooper, Charlotte, *50 Object Stories for Children,* 2523–0
Cross, Luther, *Easy Object Stories,* 2502–8
Cross, Luther, *Object Lessons for Children,* 2315–7
Cross, Luther, *Story Sermons for Children,* 2328–9
De Jonge, Joanne, *More Object Lessons from Nature,* 3004–8
De Jonge, Joanne, *Object Lessons from Nature,* 2989–9
De Jonge, Joanne, *Object Lessons from Your Home and Yard,* 3026–9
Edstrom, Lois, *Contemporary Object Lessons for Children's Church,* 3432–9
Gebhardt, Richard, & Mark Armstrong, *Object Lessons from Science Experiments,* 3811–1
Godsey, Kyle, *Object Lessons About God,* 3841–3
Hendricks, William, *Object Lessons Based on Bible Characters,* 4373–5
Hendricks, William, & Merle Den Bleyker, *Object Lessons from Sports and Games,* 4134–1
Hendricks, William, & Merle Den Bleyker, *Object Lessons That Teach Bible Truths,* 4172–4
Loeks, Mary, *Object Lessons for Children's Worship,* 5584–9
McDonald, Roderick, *Successful Object Sermons,* 6270–5
Runk, Wesley, *Object Lessons from the Bible,* 7698–6
Squyres, Greg, *Simple Object Lessons for Young Children,* 8330–3
Sullivan, Jessie, *Object Lessons and Stories for Children's Church,* 8037–1
Sullivan, Jessie, *Object Lessons with Easy-to-Find Objects,* 8190–4
Trull, Joe, *40 Object Sermons for Children,* 8831–3

Special Object Lessons
for Young Children

Greg Squyres

Baker Books

A Division of Baker Book House Co
Grand Rapids, Michigan 49516

©1995 by Greg Squyres

Published by Baker Books
a division of Baker Book House Company
P.O. Box 6287, Grand Rapids, MI 49516-6287

ISBN 0-8010-5012-X

Printed in the United States of America

Scripture is taken from the HOLY BIBLE, NEW INTERNATIONAL
VERSION®. NIV®. Copyright © 1973, 1978, 1984 by International Bible
Society. Used by permission of Zondervan Publishing House. All rights
reserved.

Contents

1

Accept One Another

Scripture: Accept one another, then, just as
Christ accepted you, in order to
bring praise to God (Rom. 15:7).

Concept: We should accept people who are
different from us.

Objects: A taco shell, a hamburger bun, and a
package of uncooked spaghetti.

 What is your favorite kind of food?
(Pause for response.) My favorite food is chicken.
How would you like it if chicken were the only kind
of food to eat in the whole world? (Pause for
response.) I don't think I would like only one kind of
food. Even if it were chicken, my favorite food, I
think I would get tired of eating the same thing every
day. It is nice to have different foods to eat. Here is a
taco shell from Mexico, spaghetti from Italy, and a
hamburger bun from the United States. I like all
these foods, even though they are different.

People are different too. People come from different places—places like Scotland, Mexico, and China.
People have different hobbies and interests. Some

like baseball, some like making crafts, and some like music. People look different. Some have blue eyes and blond hair, others have brown eyes and black hair. Some are tall, and others are short.

Foods are different, and people are different. Hamburgers aren't better than spaghetti—just different. Tacos aren't better than hamburgers—just different. And just as we enjoy all the different kinds of foods in the world, we also can enjoy all the different kinds of people in the world.

The Bible says to "accept one another." We accept tacos and spaghetti and hamburgers as all being good, although they are different. Let's accept other people as being good also, although they may be different from us.

Dear God, thank you for making us all different. Help us to accept others who are different from us. Amen.

2

Always Give Thanks

Scripture: Give thanks in all circumstances, for this is God's will for you in Christ Jesus (1 Thess. 5:18).

Concept: Be thankful even when things go wrong, because God still loves us.

Object: A quarter.

People talk about having good days and bad days. A good day is when things go right. Your mom fixes your favorite food for dinner. You get a good grade on a test at school. Your parents take you to the zoo. These are all good things, and when good things happen we call it a good day. How do you feel on good days? *(Pause for response.)*

But we also have bad days sometimes. Bad days are when things don't go right. Your brother breaks your favorite toy. Your dog runs away from home. You get sick on your birthday. These are all bad things, and when bad things happen we call it a bad day. How do you feel on bad days? *(Pause for response.)*

Our days are like this quarter. Let's say that heads stands for good days, and tails stands for bad days. As we flip the quarter, first we have heads, a good day. As we flip it again it comes up tails, a bad day. *(Repeat flipping the coin several more times, announcing whether it came up heads or tails.)* The coin didn't always come up heads, a good day. We had some heads and some tails, some good days and some bad days. That's how life is. We all have good days and bad days.

Do you think God loves us more on good days than on bad days? *(Pause for response.)* God loves us always. When we have good days, he is happy with us. When we have bad days, he understands our feelings and can help us. God's love is always the same, whether we are having a good day or a bad day.

The Bible says we are to "give thanks in all circumstances." That means that we are to thank God when we are having good days and when we are having bad days. It may seem strange to give thanks on bad days. On bad days we're not giving thanks because we are happy the dog ran away or we got sick on our birthday. We are giving thanks because God loves and cares for us. So, whether our day is good or bad, we are thankful that God loves us just the same.

Thank you, God, for your love. We thank you that whether our day is good or bad, you love and care for us. Amen.

3

The Lord's Supper

Scripture: And he took bread, gave thanks and broke it, and gave it to them, saying, "This is my body given for you; do this in remembrance of me" (Luke 22:19).

Concept: At the Lord's Supper we remember that Jesus died for our sins.

Objects: A cup of grape juice and a communion wafer. (*Note*: This object lesson is given when the church participates in the Lord's Supper.)

Today people in our church will be eating the Lord's Supper. When we eat the Lord's Supper, we drink grape juice and eat small crackers like these *(show the juice and wafer)*. It may be strange to think of eating and drinking so little at a supper. Usually when we eat a supper at home, we eat much more than this!

But the purpose of the Lord's Supper is not to get full. The purpose is to remember Jesus. Both the grape juice and the cracker remind us of Jesus. The grape juice reminds us of the blood of Jesus, and the cracker reminds us of his body. As we think about

Jesus' blood and body, we remember that he died on the cross.

Why did Jesus die on a cross? *(Pause for response.)* Jesus died for the sins of all the people in the world. What is sin? *(Pause for response.)* Sin is anything we do that displeases God. So when we do things that are wrong, we realize that Jesus died for us, too.

When we sin, we deserve to be punished. But when Jesus died on the cross, he accepted the punishment for us.

Do you think it was hard for Jesus to die on the cross? *(Pause for response.)* I think it was a very hard thing to do. But Jesus gave his life on the cross because he loves us so much. So, when Christians eat the Lord's Supper, they remember how much Jesus loves them.

Dear God, thank you for your love. Thank you for Jesus, who accepted our punishment for sin when he died on the cross. Amen.

Our Valuable Mothers

Scripture: Honor your father and mother (Matt. 19:19).

Concept: Mothers are more valuable than things such as money or diamonds.

Object: A picture of your mother. (*Note:* This lesson should be presented on Mother's Day.)

This is a picture of someone special in my life. Can you guess who she is? *(Pause for response.)* This is a picture of my mother.

Mothers are important people. Can you think of any reasons why mothers are important? *(Pause for response.)* Mothers are important because without mothers, people wouldn't be born. Every new baby that comes into the world is borne by a mother. Mothers are also important because they provide love for their children. A mother's loving hug can make a person feel good all over. Mothers are also important because they take care of their children.

They do things like cook dinners, put bandages on skinned knees, and make sure their children have taken a bath and brushed their teeth. Mothers are also important because they teach their children. When their children are young, they teach them how to feed themselves and speak. They also teach their children about God and how to know right from wrong.

Mothers are important for many reasons. The Bible says we are to honor our mothers. The Bible word for *honor* means to highly value, or prize. There are many valuable things in the world—money, diamonds, baseball cards—but of all the valuable things in the world, none is more valuable than your mother.

Dear God, thank you for our mothers. Thank you for their love and all the many things they do for us. Amen.

When Things Change

Scripture: Every good and perfect gift is from above, coming down from the Father of the heavenly lights, who does not change like shifting shadows (James 1:17).

Concept: God helps us when things change.

Objects: A color photograph and an undeveloped roll of film.

Have any of you ever taken a picture of something with a camera? *(Pause for response.)* I enjoy taking pictures, and I enjoy looking at the pictures I have taken.

Here is a picture I took. After I took this picture, I removed the roll of film from the camera and took it to the store to have it developed. I gave the store a roll of film like this, but when I went back a couple days later, I picked up a picture that looked like this. A change took place, didn't it? The roll of film changed into a picture.

Many things in life change. You change from one school grade to another each year. And as you change grades, you change teachers, also. Sometimes

15

friends move away and you make new friends. Sometimes your favorite show gets taken off television.

Some of the changes we face are good. But some of the changes may make us feel afraid, sad, or angry. We may be a little afraid as we enter a new school grade. We are sad when friends move away. We are angry when our television show gets removed.

The feelings we have are okay. It's all right to feel afraid, sad, or angry. But God can help us with our feelings. The Bible says that God never changes. He is always loving and kind and ready to listen.

So, next time something changes in your life that makes you unhappy, talk to God about it. Remember, God never changes. He will listen to you and help you feel better about the changes you face.

Dear God, thank you for listening to us when things make us unhappy and we need to talk to someone. Thank you for loving us and caring for us. Amen.

We All Are Worth Much

Scripture: So God created man in his own image (Gen. 1:27).

Concept: No matter how old we are, we are worth the same to God.

Objects: Two pennies. One should be brand-new and the other a few years old.

I have two coins. These coins were made at different times. Can anyone tell me how we know when these coins were made? *(Pause for response.)* Each coin is stamped with the year it was made. Let's look at these coins to see when they were made.

(Read the date of the first coin, the newer.) This coin is not very old at all. Can someone tell me how much this coin is worth? *(Pause for response.)* That's right; this coin is worth one cent.

(Read the date of the second coin.) This coin is a few years old. It looks older than this shiny new coin, doesn't it? How much is this coin worth? *(Pause for response.)* Yes, this coin is also worth one cent.

Both coins are worth one cent. The newer coin is worth one cent, and the coin that is a few years old is also worth one cent. The value of a penny doesn't go down just because it gets old. It is still worth the same as when it was brand-new.

People are like pennies in this way. All people are of great worth to God. A newborn baby is worth very much to God. A boy or girl your age is worth the same to God. A man or woman my age is worth much to God, also. And so is a person who is as old as your grandma or grandpa. It doesn't matter how young or how old we are. Our worth to God is always the same. Everybody is worth very much to God, and he loves us greatly.

Dear God, we thank you that all of us are important to you, no matter how old or how young we may be. Thank you, God, for loving us. Amen.

7

Count the Cost

Scripture: Suppose one of you wants to build a tower. Will he not first sit down and estimate the cost to see if he has enough money to complete it? (Luke 14:28).

Concept: We must obey Jesus in order to follow him.

Object: A price tag.

This is a price tag. A price tag is helpful because it tells us how much something costs. By looking at the price tag, we can tell if we can buy what is for sale.

Let's pretend that I have five dollars in my pocket. I go shopping at a store to buy some clothes. I find a nice pair of pants that I like, and so I take it to the cash register to pay for it. When the cashier looks at the price tag, she says it costs $59.99. But I only have five dollars! Will I be able to buy the pants? *(Pause for response.)*

Before you buy something, you must be able to pay the price. It is silly to try to buy something without first thinking about how much it costs.

Do you know that it costs something to follow Jesus? Jesus said we need to think of what it costs before we follow him. What do you think it costs to follow Jesus? *(Pause for response.)* It doesn't cost money to follow Jesus. It costs obedience. We must obey Jesus in order to follow him.

If a person says he wants to follow Jesus, but he never wants to go to church, is he obeying Jesus? *(Pause for response.)* If a person says she wants to follow Jesus, but she never wants to read the Bible, is she obeying Jesus? *(Pause for response.)* If a person says he wants to follow Jesus, but he never wants to tell anyone else about Jesus' love, is he obeying Jesus? *(Pause for response.)*

When people follow Jesus, they go to church, read the Bible, tell others about Jesus, and do anything else Jesus wants them to do. As we pray, let's ask God to help us completely obey Jesus.

Dear God, help us to do the things Jesus wants us to do. Forgive us when we don't obey him, and help us to do better. Amen.

A Place Where Nobody Cries

Scripture: He will wipe every tear from their eyes. There will be no more death or mourning or crying or pain, for the old order of things has passed away (Rev. 21:4).

Concept: There is no sadness in heaven.

Object: An onion.

Do you like onions? *(Pause for response.)* I don't like to eat onions all by themselves, but there are many foods that taste better with onions.

When I eat a hamburger, I like to put a slice of onion on it. I also enjoy a bowl of chili with some chopped onions sprinkled on top. As much as I enjoy eating onions, there is one thing I don't like to do with onions. I don't like to chop them. Do you know why? *(Pause for response.)* It is because when I cut into an onion with a knife, the onion stings my eyes and makes me cry. Has an onion ever made you cry? *(Pause for response.)*

There are many other things that can make us cry, also. What are some things that make us cry? *(Pause for response.)* Yes, we might cry when we are hurt or sad or afraid.

Do you know that there is a place where nobody ever cries? Heaven is that place. Heaven is a wonderful place that Jesus is preparing for everyone who believes in him. There won't be any crying in heaven because there won't be any pain or sadness or fear in heaven. Heaven is a place of fun and happiness.

Next time you get hurt and begin to cry, you can ask God to help you. But you can also thank God for heaven, a place where we can someday live without pain or sadness or fear.

Dear God, thank you for helping us when we cry. Thank you also for heaven, where there will be no crying, pain, or sadness. Amen.

What Dad Wants Most

Scripture: Honor your father and your mother, so that you may live long in the land the LORD your God is giving you (Exod. 20:12).

Concept: Our best gift to Dad is our love.

Object: A newspaper advertisement for a Father's Day sale. (*Note*: This lesson is given on Father's Day.)

Today is Father's Day! On Father's Day we tell Dad how special he is. One way we do that on Father's Day is to give Dad a gift. There are many things we can give our fathers. We can make something for them, we can do something special for them, or we can buy something for them from a store.

I wonder, of all the things we could give our fathers, what would they like the most? I've brought a newspaper advertisement from a store. The advertisement suggests many things that we could give Dad. Let's look through the advertisement to see if we can find the best gift for Dad.

Here on the front page is an interesting gift. It is a cordless telephone. With a cordless telephone, Dad

23

could be working outside in the garden and still have the phone right next to him. Do you think this would be the best gift we could give our fathers? *(Pause for response.)*

Oh, look! Here is something that most fathers could use. It is an electric shaver. Most fathers shave every day. An electric shaver would help Dad shave easier and faster. Do you think that this is the best gift we could give our fathers? *(Pause for response.)*

There are hundreds of different things we could give our dads. And no matter what we give them, I know they would like it. But the best thing we could give our fathers isn't in this advertisement. The best thing we could give our dads isn't sold in a store. The gift Dad wants the most from us is our love. So, no matter what you give your dad this Father's Day, remember also to give him your love today and all year long!

Dear God, thank you for our fathers. Help us every day to show them how much we love them. Amen.

Dedicated to God

Scripture: And King Solomon offered a sacrifice of twenty-two thousand head of cattle and a hundred and twenty thousand sheep and goats. So the king and all the people dedicated the temple of God (2 Chron. 7:5).

Concept: We need to live especially for Jesus.

Object: A book with a dedication page.

Books have many pages in them. Most of the pages tell the story of the book. Besides the story pages, there are other special pages inside.

When we open up a book, we see a page called a title page. *(Open the book and show the title page.)* Many books also have a page called a table of contents. *(Show the table of contents.)* This page tells us what the name of each chapter in the book is. But the special page I want us to think about today is called a dedication page. *(Show the dedication.)*

When a person writes a book, he often dedicates the book to someone. Sometimes he dedicates it to several people. *(Read the dedication page.)* Dedicating a book means that the writer has written the book especially for a person. Other people may read the book, of course. But the writer includes a dedication page to let everyone know that the person mentioned on the dedication page is very special to him.

Other things can be dedicated, also. The Bible tells us about King Solomon leading the people to build a beautiful temple to worship in. When the temple was all built, the people got together and dedicated it to God. That means God was special to the people, and the temple would be used only for God.

The most important thing we can dedicate is our lives. God wants us to dedicate our lives to Jesus. That means we live especially for Jesus and do what Jesus wants us to do. Our lives should be dedicated to Jesus. We should live so everyone can see how special he is to us.

Dear God, help us to live especially for Jesus every day. He is special to us, and we love him. Amen.

11

Caring for God's Good Earth

Scripture: The earth is the LORD's, and everything in it (Ps. 24:1).

Concept: God wants us to take good care of his creation.

Objects: An empty soda can, a lightbulb, and a toothbrush. (*Note:* This lesson is given on Earth Day.)

Today is Earth Day. On Earth Day we think about ways in which we can take better care of the earth. Why is it so important that we take care of the earth? *(Pause for response.)* There are many good reasons why we should take care of the earth. Let me tell you two of those reasons. First, God told us to take care of it. God made the earth, and he wants us to keep it in good shape. Second, we live on the earth. We should want the place where we live to be kept up as well as possible.

There are many things we can do to take better care of the earth. Do any of you like to drink sodas? *(Pause for response.)* Here is an empty soda can. What do we do with the can when the soda is all gone? *(Pause for response.)*

Many people throw the can away, and that is good. But a better thing to do is to save our cans and recycle them. Cans are made from metal, and metal comes from the earth. So, if we recycle our cans to make new cans, we won't have to take the metal from the earth.

(Hold up toothbrush.) Do you brush your teeth? *(Pause for response.)* There is something we can do to take care of the earth as we brush our teeth. We can leave the water off until it is time to rinse our mouths. Some people run the water all the time they brush their teeth, and the water just goes down the drain. If we turn on the water only when we need it, we can save water and take better care of the earth.

Another thing we can do to take better care of the earth has to do with this lightbulb. *(Hold up the lightbulb.)* Let's pretend that you are reading in your bedroom. You have the light on so that you can see better. You decide to take a break and go outside to play for a while. What should you do as you leave the room? *(Pause for response.)* We need to remember to turn off the light. Lights take energy, and energy comes from the earth. We can save energy and take better care of the earth if we remember to turn off lights we aren't using.

God has made a good world for us to live in. He told us to take care of it. Let's keep it in good shape.

Dear God, thank you for the earth you have given us to live on. Help us to do things that will take good care of the earth. Amen.

Empty Isn't Always Bad

Scripture: He is not here; he has risen, just as he said. Come and see the place where he lay (Matt. 28:6).

Concept: The empty tomb showed that Jesus was alive.

Object: A plastic hollow Easter egg. (*Note:* This lesson is given on Easter.)

Easter egg hunts are fun. It used to be there was only one kind of Easter egg—the kind we eat. But now there are also eggs like this. *(Show the plastic egg.)* They are hollow on the inside. Have any of you ever found an egg like this on an Easter egg hunt? *(Pause for response.)* What did you find inside? *(Pause for response.)*

Often there is something good inside, such as candy or a small toy or coins. We look forward to opening the egg to see what is inside because we know it will be a good surprise. But what if, when we opened the egg, it was empty? Would that be a good surprise? *(Pause for response.)* An empty Easter egg would be rather disappointing. Many things are disappointing when they are empty. An empty cookie jar isn't any fun. Have your moms or dads ever driven their car when suddenly the gas tank became empty? *(Pause for response.)* Sometimes I want a bowl of cereal for breakfast, but when I go to pour on the milk, I find the carton empty. Times like these are disappointing. But empty isn't always bad.

On the very first Easter morning, some women went to the tomb of Jesus. Jesus had died on the cross and was buried in a tomb in a garden. The women didn't expect to find anything good at the tomb. They expected to find Jesus' dead body. But when they got to the tomb, the tomb was empty. Do you think that was a good thing or a bad thing? *(Pause for response.)* It was a wonderful thing, because Jesus had come back to life and left the tomb. There was no reason for him to be in the tomb because tombs are for dead people, and Jesus was not dead!

And so although an empty Easter egg may be a disappointing surprise, the empty tomb at Easter was a wonderful surprise. We celebrate Easter today because the tomb is empty and Jesus is alive!

Dear God, thank you for Easter. We thank you that Jesus is alive and that he is our friend. Amen.

When We Fail

Scripture: I brought him to your disciples, but they could not heal him (Matt. 17:16).

Concept: God loves us even when we fail.

Object: A hard-boiled egg. Crack the shell a little during the cooking so that some of the white seeps out and the egg looks obviously imperfect.

I cooked this hard-boiled egg this morning. It doesn't look very good, does it? The problem is that I cracked the shell as I was cooking it, and so some of the egg seeped out. It looks rather ugly. It probably tastes okay, but if I were trying to cook the perfect boiled egg, I certainly failed.

We all fail sometimes. Maybe you failed a test at school, or struck out in a baseball game, or forgot a promise you made to your mom or dad.

Even Jesus' disciples failed sometimes. The Bible tells us of a time when a man had a very sick son. He brought his son to Jesus' disciples because Jesus wasn't around at the time. The disciples tried to heal the boy, but everything they tried failed. They couldn't heal him. When Jesus finally came back, he had to heal the boy himself because the disciples failed to do it.

But the great thing about Jesus is that he loves us even when we fail. When the disciples failed to heal the boy, Jesus didn't get mad and tell them they couldn't be his disciples anymore. He loved them and helped them to do better next time.

Jesus treats us the same way. When we fail, Jesus still loves us. Jesus loves us whether we win or lose.

Dear God, thank you for your love. Thank you that even when we fail you love us and help us to do better. Amen.

14

God Knows What Is on the Inside

Scripture: O LORD, you have searched me and you know me (Ps. 139:1).

Concept: God knows our feelings and can help us feel better when we're sad.

Object: An unopened package of M&M's candy.

This is one of my favorite kinds of candy. *(Hold up package of candy.)* Inside this package are chocolate candies coated with colored shells. Can you name all the colors that are in this package? *(Pause for responses.)* Let's suppose we want to know how many yellow candies are in the package. How many yellow candies do you think are in here? *(Pause for responses.)*

We can't see through the package. The only way we can know how many yellow candies are in the package is to open the package and count them. But it is fun to guess. Let's open the package and see how many yellow ones are inside. *(Open the package and count the yellow candies.)*

Do you think God knew how many yellow candies were in the package before we opened it? *(Pause for responses.)* Of course God knew, because God knows everything. God not only knows what is inside an M&M's package, but he also knows what is inside us.

God knows how we feel inside. Other people may look at us and guess what we're feeling, but God knows what is going on inside us. He knows when we are happy and when we are sad. He knows when we are discouraged, worried, or angry.

God not only knows how we feel inside, but he also cares about our feelings. The Bible says we can tell God about our feelings because he cares about us (1 Peter 5:7). When we talk to him about our feelings, he can help us feel better. Let's talk to him now.

Dear God, you know how we feel on the inside. When we are sad, lonely, discouraged, or worried, help us to tell you about those feelings. Thank you for caring about how we feel. Amen.

How to Fix a Broken Heart

Scripture: This is my command: Love each other (John 15:17).

Concept: We should help our friends when they're sad.

Object: A "Fix-It-Yourself" manual.

Maybe your dad or mom uses a book like this at home. This is a fix-it-yourself manual. A book like this tells us how to fix all kinds of things around the house. We can learn to fix a toaster, or a bicycle, or a chair, or many other things. A book like this can be very handy.

There is one thing that this book doesn't tell us how to fix. It doesn't tell us how to fix a broken heart.

You may know someone who has a broken heart. Maybe you have had a broken heart yourself at one time. What does it mean when a person has a broken heart? *(Pause for response.)* When we say a person has a broken heart, we mean that his feelings are hurt very, very badly, and he is very sad.

Let's pretend that a friend of yours has a broken heart. You would like to help your friend feel better. What could you do to help your friend who feels very sad? *(Pause for response.)*

Your ideas are very good. There are many things we could do to help a person with a broken heart. We could talk to him, write a nice note to him, make something special for him—like a batch of chocolate chip cookies—or pray for him. We try to help our friend because we love him.

Jesus tells us to love each other. Our friends especially need our love when they are sad and their hearts are broken. Nothing can fix a broken heart like love.

Thank you, God, for your love. Help us to love others, especially when they are sad and their hearts are broken. Amen.

We Can't Fool God

Scripture: For God is greater than our hearts, and he knows everything (1 John 3:20).

Concept: God knows all we do and think.

Object: A mask one might wear with a costume.

Why do people wear masks? *(Pause for response.)* People wear masks when they pretend to be someone or something they are not. When we wear a mask, we can pretend to be Frankenstein or a Teenage Mutant Ninja Turtle or a lion or president of the United States! It is fun to pretend.

Have you ever been in a costume and fooled people into not knowing who you really were? *(Pause for response.)* Part of the fun of wearing masks and costumes is fooling people. A really good costume can fool lots of people!

Do you think that when we wear masks and costumes we can fool God? *(Pause for response.)* The Bible tells us that God knows everything. Nothing is hidden from him. No matter how good our disguise might be, God is never fooled.

Pretending, by wearing a costume or a mask, can be a lot of fun. But other kinds of pretending can be bad. Let's imagine that you came to church on Sunday wearing your best clothes. You sang songs about how much you love Jesus and prayed out loud during Sunday school promising God that you would do only things that would make him happy. But then as the week went on, you got into a fight on the playground at school, cheated on a test, and lied to your mother. It's not good to act like we love God when we are in church and then disobey him when we leave church, is it? God is not fooled. He sees us at school, at home, and at play just as he sees us at church.

So, our love for God should never be something we pretend. We can show that we really love him as we live for him every day.

Dear God, help us to live for you every day. Forgive us when we do things that displease you. Amen.

17

Forgive One Another

Scripture: Bear with each other and forgive whatever grievances you may have against one another. Forgive as the Lord forgave you (Col. 3:13).

Concept: We should forgive others as Jesus forgives us.

Object: An old coffee cup with the handle broken off.

Has anyone ever done something or said something to you that hurt you? *(Pause for response.)* The Bible says we are to forgive people when they hurt us. What does it mean to forgive? *(Pause for response.)* When we forgive someone, that means that we tell the person who has hurt us that it is okay. We don't try to get back at that person. We don't keep reminding him of how much hurt he caused.

I have a coffee cup with me. There is something wrong with my cup, isn't there? The handle broke off.

Suppose you were the one who broke my cup. You felt bad for doing it. You came to me and apologized. Would you want me to tell you that I hated you for breaking my cup? *(Pause for response.)* Would you want me to tell you that you were stupid to break my cup? *(Pause for response.)* Would you want me to tell you that you broke my cup on purpose? *(Pause for response.)* When you came to apologize for breaking my cup, what would you like me to tell you? *(Pause for response.)*

God can forgive any wrong thing we do. When someone does something or says something that hurts us, we need to forgive that person, also.

Dear God, thank you for forgiving our sins. Help us to forgive others when they hurt us. Amen.

The Hardest Thing to Do

Scripture: Greater love has no one than this, that he lay down his life for his friends (John 15:13).

Concept: It was hard for Jesus to die for us.

Objects: A half dozen eggs, a large bowl, a small bowl, and a damp towel.

Today I need two people to help me. Who would like to help? *(Select two volunteers. Instruct the first volunteer as follows:)* I would like you to take one egg and crack it into this large bowl. After you crack the egg, you may put the shell into this smaller bowl and wipe off your hands with this towel. Do you understand? Okay, go ahead and crack your egg. *(Let the volunteer crack the egg.)* Was it easy or hard to crack the egg into the bowl? *(Pause for response. Next, instruct the second volunteer as follows:)* Now, I would like you also to crack an egg into the bowl, only I want you to do it a little differently. You will crack the egg into the large bowl using only one hand. I've seen great chefs crack eggs like this! After you crack the egg into the large bowl and put the shell into the small bowl, you may wipe your hands off with this towel. Do you understand? Okay, go ahead and crack the egg. *(Let the volunteer crack the egg.)* Was that easy or hard to do? *(Pause for response.)*

(Now address all the children.) Which do you think was harder to do, cracking the egg with two hands or with one? *(Pause for response.)* There are some things that are very easy to do, and there are some things that are hard to do. For most children, counting to ten is easy, but counting to a thousand is hard. Most children find it easy to ride a bicycle or tricycle, but they would find it hard to drive a car.

When Jesus was on earth, he did some things that were easy and some things that were hard. It was easy for Jesus to tell other people about God's love. He liked talking with people, so he found this easy. Also, I think that the miracles Jesus did were easy for him, although they would be very hard for us.

But one thing was very hard for Jesus to do. It was hard for Jesus to die on the cross. Dying on the cross was the hardest thing anybody has ever done. Jesus, who had never done anything wrong, died on the cross for all the wrong things everybody else did.

Jesus died on the cross because he loves us. The Bible says there is no greater love than for someone to give his life for his friends. We are Jesus' friends. So although it was a hard thing to do, Jesus loved us enough to give his life on the cross.

Dear God, thank you for the love of Jesus. Thank you that he loved us so much that he died on the cross for us. Amen.

God Hears Us

Scripture: Does he who implanted the ear not hear? (Ps. 94:9).

Concept: God hears us when we pray.

Object: A garden hose. In advance of the lesson, drain the hose of all water.

Today we are going to do something I used to have fun doing when I was a little boy. First, I need a volunteer. *(Choose a child.)* I need you to take the end of this hose and stretch it out as far as it will go. Then, put the end of the hose to your ear, and I will speak to you through the hose. *(Have the child follow your directions, and carry on a short conversation with him. Then, have him rejoin the other children.)*

That's pretty amazing. We can speak through a garden hose that is fifty feet long, and someone on the other end can hear us as if we were right next to him. Even if we whispered through the hose, it could be heard fifty feet away at the other end.

But far more amazing is the way in which God hears our prayers. It makes no difference where we are or when we pray. It doesn't matter if we shout or if we whisper. God hears our prayers. He hears them every time. He even hears our prayers when we don't pray out loud. And God doesn't need a garden hose or a walkie-talkie or a telephone or anything else to hear us. God hears us because he is God. He hears and knows everything.

So, whenever we need to talk to God, we don't need to worry whether or not he is close enough to hear. God is always close enough, and he always hears our prayers. Let's pray to him now.

Dear God, thank you for always hearing our prayers. You are good to us, and we love you. Amen.

Hear and Obey

Scripture: He replied, "Blessed rather are those who hear the word of God and obey it" (Luke 11:28).

Concept: We must obey the Bible, not just hear it.

Objects: A tape recorder and a cassette tape of the Bible (or record a chapter or two of the Bible on tape yourself).

I've got something on this tape I want you to hear. *(Play a few verses of the Bible on tape.)* Can anyone tell me what we have been listening to on this tape? *(Pause for response.)* Yes, this is a tape of the Bible.

Having a tape of the Bible is a good idea. It can be used in many ways. Children might be too young to read the Bible by themselves, but by playing it on this tape, they can hear the Bible. Or people who are blind and unable to read a written Bible can hear the Bible on tape. People driving in their car can't read the Bible while they are driving, but they can play the tape in their car tape player. So, even while they are driving, they can hear the Bible.

It is good to hear the Bible, because the Bible is God's Word to us. When we hear the Bible, we learn what God wants us to do and how he wants us to live.

But hearing the Bible is not enough. It is only the beginning of what God wants us to do. Jesus said "Blessed (*or* happy) are those who hear the word of God and obey it." Once we have heard what God wants us to do in the Bible, we must obey what the Bible says.

Let's pretend a boy went to Sunday school and heard his teacher read from the Bible. The verse she read was "You shall not steal." After he heard the verse, he went home, went into his sister's room, and stole a quarter. Was hearing the Bible enough? *(Pause for response.)* No, it is never enough just to hear the Bible. To please God we must not only hear the Bible, but also obey it.

Dear God, thank you for the Bible. Help us not only to hear your word to us, but also to obey it. Amen.

21

Jesus Loves Us

Scripture: But God demonstrates his own love for us in this: While we were still sinners, Christ died for us (Rom. 5:8).

Concept: Jesus shows his love in many ways, but mostly by dying for us.

Object: A can of cherry pie filling.

This is a can of cherry pie filling. Since I was a little boy, cherry has been one of my favorite kinds of pie. I remember going to my grandma's house. If she knew I was coming, she often would bake a cherry pie. She made delicious cherry pies! I felt special when Grandma made a cherry pie for me.

When I first met my wife, Judy, she wanted to do something special for me. She found out that cherry was my favorite pie, so do you know what she did? *(Pause for response.)* Yes, Judy baked a cherry pie for me. It is a pie that I will never forget! And now, when she wants to do something special for me, she will often bake something for me, like a pie, cookies, or cake. Judy doesn't bake things for me because she has to. She bakes for me because she loves me.

Our moms and dads do things for us all the time to show us they love us. What are some things your mom and dad do for you because they love you? *(Pause for response.)* They don't do these things because they *have* to, but because they *love* you.

Jesus does things for us, too, because he loves us. What are some things that Jesus does for us to show us his love? *(Pause for response.)* Yes, Jesus does many things for us. The Bible says that the greatest thing Jesus did for us was to die on the cross for our sins. But one thing we need to remember about Jesus dying on the cross: He didn't die on the cross because he had to. He did it to show how much he loves us.

Jesus did not stay dead. He came back to life. He now is living in heaven. He promised that someday we can live there with him if we believe that he is God's Son and we ask him to forgive us our sins.

Dear God, thank you for all the things you do for us because you love us. Most of all, we thank you for Jesus, who loved us so much he died on the cross for our sins. And we thank you that someday we can live with you and Jesus in heaven. Amen.

Our Home in Heaven

Scripture: In my Father's house are many
rooms; if it were not so, I would have told
you (John 14:2).

Concept: Heaven is a special place where we
can live forever.

Object: The real estate section of a newspaper.

If you wanted to buy a new house, you probably would look in the newspaper. The newspaper
has a section in it that describes houses for sale. Here's
one house that looks pretty good. *(Read the description of the house.)* Does that sound like a good house
to you? *(Pause for response.)* Here's another house for
sale. *(Read the description of the second house.)*

Houses are different. Some houses are big. Others
are small. Some houses have an upstairs and a down-
stairs. Others have only one level. Some houses are
made of wood. Others are made of brick or stone.

Some Eskimos live in a house made of snow called
an igloo. Some people in Africa live in grass huts.
Igloos and grass huts are different kinds of houses.

Some houses are very fancy. Fancy houses are called mansions. The White House where the president lives is a mansion. It is a huge house with many rooms. Mansions are very expensive homes, so only very rich people live in them.

People don't live in houses forever. That is because people don't live forever, and even if they did, the houses wouldn't last forever. But there is a place where we can live forever. It is a place Jesus is preparing for us. It is a place called heaven.

Heaven is a very special place. Jesus is preparing a home there for everyone who believes in him. In heaven, people live forever. And the homes Jesus is making in heaven will last forever.

There are no houses on earth that can compare with heaven: not an igloo, a grass hut, a mansion, or any of the houses in this newspaper. Heaven is a place so special that we can't even imagine how great it will be.

But the best thing about heaven is that we will live forever with Jesus. Jesus loves us and wants to live forever with us. We can live someday with him in heaven if we love and trust in him.

Dear God, thank you for heaven, the special place where we can live someday. We thank you that Jesus is there and we can live with him someday. Amen.

23

How to Think of Others

Scripture: Do nothing out of selfish ambition or vain conceit, but in humility consider others better than yourselves (Phil. 2:3).

Concept: We should be kind to others and not act as if we're better than they are.

Objects: Enough paper crowns to give one to each child.

I have something for each of you. *(Distribute crowns and ask children to put their crowns on their heads.)* Each of us is wearing a crown. What kind of people wear crowns? *(Pause for response.)* Kings and queens and other very important people wear crowns, don't they?

The crowns we are wearing are paper, but let's pretend that our crowns are made of pure gold and each crown has a hundred diamonds on it. That would be a very expensive crown. How would you feel wearing a crown like that? *(Pause for response.)*

Wearing a very expensive crown might make some people feel as if they are better than other people. Is it wrong to feel as if you are better than other people? *(Pause for response.)*

The Bible says that we are to think of others as better than ourselves. That means that we are not to go around bragging about how good we are, or picking on kids that are smaller than we are, or making fun of other people. We are to treat others with kindness.

Wearing a paper crown is fun. But acting as if we are better than other people is not fun. It hurts other people's feelings.

Does God hurt people's feelings? *(Pause for response.)* God doesn't hurt people's feelings, because he is kind toward all people. Kindness makes people feel good. As we learn to be more like God, we treat all people with kindness, too.

Dear God, thank you for your kindness. Help us to treat others in the same kind way you treat us. Amen.

24

The Good News Is Up-to-Date

Scripture: Then I saw another angel flying in mid-air, and he had the eternal gospel to proclaim to those who live on the earth— to every nation, tribe, language and people (Rev. 14:6).

Concept: The Bible is never out-of-date.

Objects: An outdated newspaper and a Bible.

This is a newspaper. A newspaper tells us what is going on in our city and around the world. Many people read a newspaper every day. Why do you think people read it every day? *(Pause for response.)*

Every newspaper has a date on the front of it. The date tells us when the newspaper was written. Let's find the date on this newspaper. *(Read the date.)* This newspaper was written quite a while ago. If you had a choice of reading a newspaper written today or this newspaper written a long time ago, which one would you choose? *(Pause for response.)* We would probably choose the newspaper written today, because it tells us things that have happened lately. The other newspaper is older. When newspapers get old they are called out-of-date.

I also have a Bible with me today. The Bible is sometimes called the gospel. The gospel means the good news. It tells the good news about Jesus.

We have discovered that a newspaper can get out-of-date. That is why we read a new one every day. Do we have to read a new Bible every day, too? *(Pause for response.)* The Bible never gets out-of-date. The Bible you read today you can read tomorrow. You can read the same Bible fifty years from now. The reason is that the gospel, the good news of Jesus, never is old. It is just as important today as it was hundreds of years ago.

Dear God, thank you for the Bible. Thank you for giving us a book so special that it never gets out-of-date. Amen.

The Cross Is Not a Joke

Scripture: For the message of the cross is foolishness to those who are perishing, but to us who are being saved it is the power of God (1 Cor. 1:18).

Concept: The cross shows Jesus' love for us and should be taken seriously.

Object: A joke book for children.

Do you like jokes? *(Pause for response.)* Good! I brought a joke book with me today. Would you like to hear a few jokes? *(Pause for response.)* Okay, I'll tell you some. *(Read a few jokes from your joke book.)*

Did you like those jokes? *(Pause for response.)* Jokes are fun because they make us laugh. They are usually silly and are not to be taken seriously.

The Bible says that some people think that the cross that Jesus died on is a joke. They laugh at it and don't take it seriously. They think that Jesus' dying on the cross was a foolish thing.

But for those who believe in Jesus the cross isn't foolish at all. When Jesus died on the cross he died for our sins—for any wrong we have ever done. And if we believe in Jesus, he has promised that we can live forever with him in heaven.

There are many funny jokes that we can laugh about. But the cross of Jesus is not a funny joke. It is Jesus' way of showing how much he loves us.

Dear God, thank you that Jesus died on the cross for our sins. Thank you for loving us so much. Amen.

26

God Loves Us
without the Labels

Scripture: I trust in God's unfailing love
for ever and ever (Ps. 52:8).

Concept: God loves us for who we are.

Object: A pair of athletic shoes with a
designer label.

I have a pair of tennis shoes with me today. Is there anything special about these shoes? *(Pause for response.)* Many people think shoes like these are special because of the name on the shoe. The maker of the shoe puts his name on it. Some people think certain names are very special.

In fact, some people will buy a pair of shoes not because the material is good, or because they look nice, or because the color is pretty, or because they are comfortable, or because they will last a long time. Some people buy shoes just because the shoe has a certain name on it.

Sometimes people will buy clothes with a certain name because they feel that their friends will like them more if they wear the right brands. Isn't that silly, that people might like you more if you wear shoes or a jacket with a certain name on it? But that's the way people are sometimes.

But God is not like that. We don't have to wear clothes that have a certain label, for God to love us. We can't impress God by wearing tennis shoes that have a fancy name. God knows all about us. He knows the good and the bad about us. And God loves us just for who we are. He doesn't like everything we do, because sometimes we do things that are wrong. But God loves us without our having to impress him. God loves us without the labels.

Thank you, God, for loving us. Thank you that we don't have to do silly things to make you love us. You know us, and you love us for who we are. Amen.

27

God Helps Us Not to Be Afraid

Scripture: The LORD is my light and my salvation—whom shall I fear? (Ps. 27:1).

Concept: As the light is a comfort, so is God.

Object: A night-light.

This is a special kind of light. It is called a night-light. When I was a little boy, I would sometimes spend the night at my grandmother's house. When it was time for me to go to bed, Grandma would get a place ready for me to sleep in the den. She would tuck me in, and just before turning off the light she would point to a night-light that was plugged into the wall and say, "There's a light for you to help you go to sleep and to keep you from getting scared."

Being in the dark all alone is scary sometimes, and a night-light like this helps. It makes us feel better to have a light when the room is dark.

The Bible says that God is a light. David wrote, "The LORD is my light and my salvation—whom shall I fear?" God is called a light because he can help us when we get scared, just like a light helps us. When we trust in God, it is like having a night-light in a dark room—things aren't as scary anymore. And so when you become afraid, remember that God is there with you. He is your light, and he can help you not to be afraid.

Thank you, God, for being with us when we are afraid. Help us always to trust in you. Amen.

28

God Loves Us First

Scripture: We love because he first loved us
(1 John 4:19).

Concept: God loved us first and shows us
about love. We should then love others.

Objects: A picture of you and your spouse
holding one of your children when he or
she was a baby.

This picture is very special to me. It is a picture of my wife and me and someone else. Can anyone tell me who the other person in the picture is? *(Pause for response.)* The other person is my son, Robert. Robert was just a little baby when this picture was made. He has grown a lot and doesn't look like a baby anymore.

I have a question for you to think about: Who loved first? Do you think that baby Robert loved me and his mother first, or do you think his mother and I loved baby Robert first? *(Pause for response.)* Robert's mother and I loved him first. In fact, Robert didn't know how to love until we showed him what love was all about.

There were many ways that we showed Robert about love. We bought food for him and fed him when he was hungry. We put clothes on him to keep him warm. We held him, talked to him, and played with him. Every day Robert learned more about love. He learned very well, because now he loves us very much.

Now I will ask you another question. Who loved first: Did you love God first, or did he love you first? *(Pause for response.)* The Bible says that God loved us first. Just like your mother and father, God loves you and shows you what love is all about. He shows us some things about love that even our mothers and fathers can't show us, because God's love is perfect. After God shows us how to love, we can love other people. We love them by praying for them, helping them, and being kind. God is pleased when we love others.

Dear God, thank you for showing us what love is all about. Help us to love others. Amen.

29

Trusting God

Scripture: But I trust in You, O LORD;
I say, You are my God (Ps. 31:14).

Concept: When we trust in God, we believe
that everything he says is true.

Object: An unopened box of facial tissues.

How many tissues are in this box? *(Pause for response.)* How do you know there are 175 tissues? *(Pause for response.)* Yes, the box says that there are 175 tissues inside. Since we haven't opened the box and used any of the tissues, we believe there are 175 tissues inside, just as the box says.

But have you ever opened a box of tissues and counted every tissue to make sure that there really were as many tissues as the box said there were? *(Pause for response.)* I haven't done that either. When I buy a box of tissues, I believe that the box contains what it says it contains. I trust the box to tell the truth about what is on the inside.

Trust means we believe something to be true. Since we believe this box to contain 175 tissues, we trust in what the box says. We believe what it says to be true.

Trusting in God means we believe God to be true and that everything he says is truth. Where do we find things that God said? *(Pause for response.)* Yes, we find what God says as we read the Bible. If we trust in God, then we believe the Bible, because the Bible is from God. It is his word to us.

It doesn't matter much whether or not you trust a box of tissues. But it matters greatly whether or not you trust in God. Trusting in God is the only way to be truly happy and the only way to someday live with God in heaven.

Dear God, help us to trust in you. Amen.

30

We Can't Measure God's Love

Scripture: The LORD, the LORD, the compassionate and gracious God, slow to anger, abounding in love and faithfulness, maintaining love to thousands, and forgiving wickedness, rebellion and sin (Exod. 34:6–7).

Concept: No tool can measure love, but God's love is too great to be measured anyway.

Objects: A measuring cup, a pitcher of water, a ruler, and a bathroom scale.

Today I have three tools used to measure things. *(Show the children the tools.)* Most things in the world can be measured with the right tool. Let's imagine that we were going to make some lemonade, and the recipe asked for two cups of water. Which of these tools would we use to measure the water? *(Pause for response.)* Yes, we would use the measuring cup. Let's measure two cups of water to see how the measuring cup works. *(Appoint a volunteer to help you measure two cups of water from the pitcher.)*

Now let's imagine that you were in school, and your teacher asked you to cut a piece of paper into a square with all the sides equaling four inches. What tool would you use to measure the paper? *(Pause for response.)* The ruler would measure the paper quite nicely. *(Demonstrate measuring the paper to make the square.)*

Now let's imagine that your grandmother came over to visit. She looked at you and said, "My, how much you have grown! How much do you weigh now?" What tool would you use to measure your weight? *(Pause for response.)* The scale measures our weight. *(Demonstrate the scale by weighing one of the boys or girls.)*

Imagine now that we were reading about God's love in the Bible. We wanted to measure how much God loves us. What tool would we use to measure God's love? *(Pause for response.)* There is no tool that can measure love. The ruler can't measure it, the measuring cup can't measure it, and the scale can't measure it. Nothing can measure love. But even if there were a tool that could measure love, God's love is so great that it cannot be measured. God loves us more than we can even imagine.

Dear God, thank you for your love for us. We love you, too. Help us to live for you every day. Amen.

31

How Important Is Money?

Scripture: And God raised us up with Christ and seated us with him in the heavenly realms in Christ Jesus, in order that in the coming ages he might show the incomparable riches of his grace, expressed in his kindness to us in Christ Jesus (Eph. 2:6–7).

Concept: Love is more important than money.

Object: A dollar bill.

D o you know what this is? *(Hold up the dollar. Pause for response.)* This is a dollar. Is money important? *(Pause for response.)* Yes, money is important. With money we can buy things that we need, such as food to eat and clothes to wear. We can also buy things that we want, such as a new bicycle or toy.

Money is important, but it is not the most important thing. Love is more important than money. The love we receive from our mothers and fathers and grandpas and grandmas is very special. It cannot be bought with money.

Is money more important than Jesus? *(Pause for response.)* Jesus is more important than all the money in the world. Jesus loves us more than anybody else can. And no amount of money can buy the joy and happiness that Jesus can give us—not a hundred dollars, not a thousand dollars, not a million dollars!

And so although money is important, it is not the most important thing in the world. We should not love money more than we love people, and we should not love money more than we love Jesus. Jesus loves us more than all the money we can imagine.

Dear God, thank you for your love. Help us to love you more than anything else in all the world. Amen.

32

The Name of Jesus

Scripture: She will give birth to a son, and you are to give him the name Jesus, because he will save his people from their sins (Matt. 1:21).

Concept: "Jesus" means "The Lord saves." Jesus saves us from our sins.

Object: The nameplate from your desk, or a name tag. (*Note:* If name tag, change first paragraph.)

This is called a nameplate. It sits on the desk in my office. When people come to my office, they see the nameplate. If they don't know my name, they can read the nameplate and know right away what my name is.

All of us are given a name when we are born. Moms and dads often think a long time before naming their baby. They want the name to be special.

Sometimes parents choose a name because the name sounds pretty. I think the name "Judy" is a very pretty name. Parents may also choose to name their baby after someone else. A boy may be given the same name as his father. Some babies are named after famous people, such as movie stars or presidents.

When Jesus was born, Mary and Joseph, his earthly parents, gave him a special name. They named him "Jesus" because that is the name God told them to give the baby. The name "Jesus" is a very special name. It means, "The Lord saves."

The Bible says that Jesus saves us from our sins. Sin is anything we do or say that displeases God.

Have you ever done anything wrong? *(Pause for response.)* I have, too. And I've been punished for doing bad things.

When we sin against God, we deserve to be punished by God. But if we believe in Jesus, Jesus saves us from the punishment we deserve.

That is a wonderful thing Jesus does for us. Whenever we think of the name "Jesus" we can remember what his name means: "The Lord saves." Jesus saves us from our sins.

Dear God, Thank you for Jesus, who saves us from our sins. Forgive us when we do or say things that displease you, and help us to do better. Amen.

33

When God Answers No

Scripture: Ask and it will be given to you; seek and you will find; knock and the door will be opened to you (Matt. 7:7).

Concept: God tells us no when what we ask for may not be good for us.

Objects: An apple and a sharp knife.

Today I have two objects with me, an apple and a knife. First let's talk about the apple. If you want this apple, what must you do to receive it? *(Pause for response.)* You must ask for the apple in order to receive it. Who would like to ask for this apple? *(Select one volunteer. Have him or her ask for the apple.)* Yes, you may have this apple. I'm very happy to give you an apple, because apples are good for you. *(Give him or her the apple.)*

Now, let's talk about the knife. If you want this knife, what must you do to receive it? *(Pause for response.)* You must ask for the knife, just as you asked for the apple. Who would like to ask for the knife? *(Select one volunteer. Have him or her ask for the knife.)* No, you may not have the knife. You might hurt yourself with the knife, so I will not let you have it.

Sometimes when we ask for things we are told no. We do not always know why we are told no, but there usually is a very good reason.

When we pray to God, the Bible says we may ask him whatever we want. But sometimes God tells us no. He tells us no when the thing we ask for is not what is best for us. If I gave one of you this sharp knife knowing it might hurt you, then I probably wouldn't care very much about you. But since I care what happens to you, I won't give you the knife. In the same way, God sometimes must tell us no. He tells us no because sometimes what we ask for may not be good for us. He cares too much about us to let us have everything we want, good or bad. God wants only the best for us.

Dear God, help us to understand when you must tell us no. Thank you for wanting only the best for us. Amen.

34

Sincere Love

Scripture: If you love me, you will obey what I command (John 14:15).

Concept: We show our love for Jesus is real by obeying him.

Objects: An artificial rose and a real rose.

These two flowers look much the same, but they are actually quite different. Can anybody tell me what is different about these two flowers? *(Pause for response.)* One of the flowers is a real rose. The other flower is fake.

Fake flowers pretend to be real flowers. They look very much like real flowers. Sometimes it is difficult to tell them apart from real flowers unless you look very closely.

What are some ways we can tell a fake flower from a real flower? *(Pause for response. Possible answers might be that they feel different, don't smell pretty, or look a little different.)* What if someone gave you this flower *(hold up the artificial rose)* and told you it was a real rose? Would you be fooled? *(Pause for response.)*

We would not be fooled, because there are ways to tell the fake flower from the real flower.

Do you know that there is also a way to show Jesus that our love for him is real? We wouldn't want Jesus to think we were just pretending to love him, would we? We want Jesus to know that we love him with all our heart. The way we show Jesus we love him is by obeying him. Jesus said, "If you love me, you will obey what I command." So, it is important that we obey what Jesus tells us to do in the Bible.

Let's show Jesus that we really love him with all our hearts. Jesus loves us very, very much. Let's show him how much we love him, too.

Dear God, thank you for loving us. We love you, too. Help us show our love for you as we obey your rules in the Bible. Amen.

35

Once Is Enough

Scripture: Whoever drinks the water I give him will never thirst (John 4:14).

Concept: Once we ask Jesus into our lives, we never have to ask again.

Object: A large glass or a thirty-two-ounce sipper.

Do you ever get thirsty? *(Pause for response.)* What do you like to drink when you get really thirsty? *(Pause for response.)* A great big cup like this could quench your thirst for a long time, couldn't it?

But even a great big cup like this gets empty. It can't quench our thirst forever. What do we have to do when the cup gets empty? *(Pause for response.)* That's right. We must fill it up again.

There are many things we have to do over again, like filling up the cup. Everybody takes a bath or a shower. But just taking one bath or shower in our lifetime is not enough. When we get dirty, we have to take another bath. When we get hungry, we eat. But a few hours later we have to eat again. One meal will never last us a lifetime.

But there is one thing we can do that we will never have to do again. We can ask Jesus to forgive our sins and be the boss of our lives. Jesus promised that when we ask him into our lives, he is there to stay. We don't have to ask him back again, because he will never leave us.

A big cup like this will get empty many times. We will have to fill it up again and again and again. But when we ask Jesus into our lives, we will never have to do it again, because he is there to stay.

Dear God, thank you for Jesus. We thank you that he is always with us when we ask him into our lives. Amen.

36

God Made the World

Scripture: In the beginning God created the heavens and the earth (Gen. 1:1).

Concept: We should remember that God made the world.

Object: A painting with the artist's signature.

I have a painting with me. It is a very beautiful painting. The artist used many different colors to paint on the canvas what he imagined in his mind.

Do you know how to tell who painted this picture? *(Pause for response.)* This painting, like most paintings, has the name of the artist in the corner of it. *(Locate the artist's name on the painting and read the name to the children.)* The artist paints his name there so that everyone who looks at the painting will know that he painted it. Each painting that an artist does is very special to him, and he is pleased to put his name on it so that people can admire and enjoy his work.

Just as an artist made this painting and the painting is special to him, God made the world, and the world is special to God. God didn't put his name on every tree, mountain, or star that he made. But the Bible tells us that "In the beginning God created the heavens and the earth."

Let's pretend that I liked this painting very much. I took some paint and crossed out the artist's name and painted in my own name instead. I was going to act as if I, not the artist, painted the painting. How do you think the artist would feel about my saying that I painted this painting? *(Pause for response.)*

I don't think the artist would be very pleased, because he painted it and it is very special to him. In the same way, I don't think God is pleased when some people pretend that he didn't make the world. God did make the world, and the world is very special to him. So let's always remember to thank God for the good world he has made.

Dear God, thank you for making the world. Everything you make is beautiful. Amen.

37

It Is Hard to Wait

Scripture: I patiently waited for the LORD;
he turned to me and heard my cry
(Ps. 40:1).

Concept: Waiting teaches us patience.

Object: A cereal box with an offer on the back
in which a person must send away for an
item.

When I was a boy I ate a lot of cereal. As I ate my cereal I would read the back of the cereal box. The back of this cereal box has a special offer. It says that if we send the cereal company two UPC symbols from the bottom of the box, we can get a hip pouch.

That's pretty cool, isn't it? But there's one catch. It says that if we send away for the hip pouch, we must allow sixty days for delivery. The hip pouch will not come in the mail the next day, or even a week after we send away for it. We must wait sixty days for it to come!

Do you like to wait? *(Pause for response.)* Most people do not like to wait. But waiting can actually be good for us.

Jesus promised that someday he will come back to earth. When he does, he will take all the people who believe in him to heaven. In the meantime, we wait for him to come back. It is not easy to wait for Jesus, because we want to see him.

One reason Jesus makes us wait is to teach us to be patient. What does "patient" mean? *(Pause for response.)* A person who is patient has learned to wait for things without getting angry or worried.

It is not easy to be patient. It is not easy to wait sixty days for our hip pouch to arrive from the cereal company. It is not easy to wait for Jesus to come back to earth. But it is good to be patient. The Bible says that Jesus is patient. So, as we learn to be more patient, we become more like Jesus.

Dear God, thank you for being patient. When we have to wait, help us to be patient, too. Amen.

38

Perfume for Jesus

Scripture: A woman came to him with an alabaster jar of very expensive perfume, which she poured on his head as he was reclining at the table (Matt. 26:7).

Concept: We should give our best to Jesus.

Object: A bottle of perfume.

This is a bottle of perfume. Women like to wear perfume because perfume smells very nice.

Some kinds of perfume don't cost very much money. But some kinds of perfume cost a lot of money. A bottle this size might cost more than one hundred dollars!

The Bible tells a story about a woman who came to Jesus one day as he was eating lunch. She had a bottle of perfume with her—*very* expensive perfume. As she came up to Jesus, what do you think she did? *(Pause for response.)* She poured the whole bottle of perfume on Jesus' head!

Jesus' disciples got mad when they saw what the woman had done. They felt that the bottle of perfume was too expensive to pour on Jesus' head. They thought the woman was wasting the perfume.

But Jesus wasn't angry. He was pleased. He told the disciples that the woman had done a very good thing. She had given her best perfume to Jesus.

Jesus' disciples learned an important lesson that day. It is a lesson we need to learn, too. The lesson is this: Jesus is pleased when we give him our best.

Our worship to Jesus should be the best. When we sing to Jesus, we should sing with our best voices. Our service for Jesus should be the best. When we help people, we should help them the best we can. And our behavior should be the best, too. As we talk or play with others, we should be kind, just as Jesus is kind.

We should never give Jesus the crummy stuff that we can do without. Instead, we always should give our best to Jesus, because he gives his best to us!

Dear God, thank you for giving us Jesus to be our friend and Savior. He is the best you had to give to us. Help us also to always give our best to you. Amen.

39

God Knows Us Personally

Scripture: O LORD, you have searched me
and you know me (Ps. 139:1).

Concept: God knows all about each of us; we
should know him, too.

Object: A personal letter written to you.

Every day I check my mailbox to see what the mail carrier has left me. Some days I get advertisements from stores. Sometimes I find bills from the gas or electric company reminding me it is time to pay them. But the mail I like to get the most comes from people I know.

Here is a letter that was written to me by a friend. Notice that the letter has my name on it. The person who wrote me this letter knows me by my name. Letters like this are called personal mail. They are letters written to us by someone who knows us as a person.

The gas company does not really know me as a person. They put my name on the bill, but that doesn't mean they know me. They don't know how old I am, or what my favorite TV show is, or what I do for fun. Those are the kinds of things a friend knows about me. Those are personal things.

A wonderful thing about God is that he knows us as a person. He knows each one of us by our names. He not only knows our names, but he also knows all about us. He knows what we like and what we don't like. He knows what makes us happy and what makes us sad. He knows when we do what is right and when we do what is wrong. He knows us just as a best friend knows us, because God is our friend.

God knows us well, and he wants us to get to know him well, too. How can we get to know God? *(Pause for response.)* Yes, we get to know God by going to Sunday school and church, by reading the Bible, by talking to him in prayer, and by getting to know Jesus, his Son. It is a great thing that God, who made the world and everything in it, knows each one of us as a personal friend.

Dear God, thank you for knowing us and loving us. Thank you for being our friend. Amen.

40

Solving Problems

Scripture: Who endowed the heart with wisdom or gave understanding to the mind? (Job 38:36).

Concept: God helps us solve our problems.

Objects: A baseball and glove. Put the items in a paper sack or box.

I have an item in this box that you have probably seen before. *(Display box. Take baseball from the box.)* Can anyone tell me what this is? *(Pause for response.)* This is a baseball. Most people know what a baseball is. You have probably played baseball or watched someone else play.

Let's pretend that nobody had ever heard of the game of baseball. You made up the game yourself and were going to teach others to play. So there you were, playing in the first baseball game ever. The pitcher threw the ball, and the batter hit it hard right toward you. You knew that to get the batter out you must stop the ball. But when you tried to stop it with your bare hands, it hurt! It hurt so badly that you thought maybe your hand was broken.

Something had to be done about this problem. Baseball was a fun game, but it hurt too much to catch the ball. Now think: If you invented the game of baseball, what might you do to solve the problem of the hurt hand? *(Pause for response.)*

(Take the baseball glove from the box.) Somebody, somewhere, invented the baseball glove. He or she probably invented it for the same reason we talked about: It hurts too much to catch a baseball with a bare hand. So, the glove protects the hand. We solved the problem, didn't we?

The Bible says that God gave us hearts with wisdom and minds that can understand things. We solved a problem with our minds just now. There are many problems in life. Some are very easy to solve, others are very difficult. But God doesn't want us to worry about problems or give up when we have a problem. He gave us good minds to solve problems. Many problems we can solve by thinking about them.

There are some problems that we might think and think about but not be able to solve. When that happens, we know God will help us with them. God loves us and cares about every problem that we may have.

Dear God, thank you for giving us good minds to think through our problems. And thank you for helping us with all the problems we can't solve. Amen.

41

All Things Work for Good

Scripture: And we know that in all things God works for the good of those who love him, who have been called according to his purpose (Rom. 8:28).

Concept: God makes good and bad days necessary in our life.

Object: A jigsaw puzzle in the original box.

Can anyone tell me what this is? *(Do not let the children see the picture of the completed puzzle on the box. Hold up one piece of the puzzle. Pause for response.)* This is a piece of a puzzle. This puzzle has five hundred pieces. When all the pieces are put together correctly, it makes a picture. Have any of you ever put together a puzzle like this? *(Pause for response.)*

Look carefully at this piece of the puzzle. Can you tell me what the picture will be by looking at this one piece? *(Pause for response.)* It is very difficult to know what the picture will be by only seeing one piece. We need every piece of the puzzle to finish the picture.

This piece of the puzzle reminds me of each day of our lives. Some days are very happy. We enjoy happy days. But some days are sad. We may wonder why we must have the sad days. We may think it isn't fair to have sad days.

But each day is necessary in our lives, just as each piece of this puzzle is necessary to make a picture. We may not know how sad days fit into our lives, just as we may wonder how this one piece fits into the finished puzzle.

But God sees beyond today. He sees our whole lives—from beginning to end. And God knows how each day fits—happy and sad. And the Bible tells us that even the sad days help to make our lives good. So, we can thank God for each happy day, and ask God to help us through the sad days.

Dear God, thank you for each day we live. Thank you for the happy days. Help us when our days are sad. Amen.

42

God Keeps Us Safe

Scripture: The LORD is my light and my salvation—whom shall I fear? (Ps. 27:1).

Concept: God keeps us from danger.

Object: A flashlight.

I have a flashlight. In dark places, a flashlight comes in handy. A flashlight is unlike many other kinds of light, because we can carry the flashlight with us. When I was a boy, our family would sometimes go camping in the summer. We would camp in the mountains, far away from the city. There would be no street light or house lights. When night came, it became very, very dark. Dad would light a lantern, and we would stay near the light that shone from it.

Sometimes, though, we had to walk away from the light of the lantern to look for more firewood for the campfire. As we walked away from the lantern, it would get darker and darker. That's when a flashlight was very helpful. Without a flashlight, we couldn't see where we were going. On a very dark path, we might trip and fall or bump into something. It would be easy to get hurt when it was so dark.

But the flashlight helped us see where we were going. It lit up the path, and we would not get hurt. The light of the flashlight kept us safe.

The Bible says that God is our light. That means he helps us to know where we are going and keeps us from danger. Just as the flashlight lights a path and keeps us from hurting ourselves, so God can keep us safe every day as we trust in him.

A flashlight can make us feel better on a dark night. But much better than a flashlight is our trust in God, who watches over us and keeps us safe.

Dear God, thank you for helping us safely through each day. Amen.

43

The Seasons of Life

Scripture: There is a time for everything, and a season for every activity under heaven (Eccles. 3:1).

Concept: God is with us through all the seasons and all the changes in our lives.

Objects: Several dried leaves. (*Note:* This lesson is given during the fall.)

These dead, dry leaves were out on the lawn at my house. They had fallen from the tree. When you see leaves like this, what do they remind you of? *(Pause for response.)* Leaves like this remind me that fall is here.

God has given us four different seasons to enjoy. There is the season of winter. What happens during winter? *(Pause for response.)* In winter, it rains a lot and sometimes snows. Then there is the season of spring. What happens in spring? *(Pause for response.)* In spring the flowers begin to bloom again, and the grass turns green. Following spring comes summer. What happens during summer? *(Pause for response.)* In summer the days get hot as the sun shines bright. And finally comes the season we are in now, fall. What happens in fall? *(Pause for response.)* In fall the weather cools down again and leaves fall from the trees.

During which season do you think God is closer to us? *(Pause for response.)* God is with us through all the seasons. He is not closer to us in summer than he is in winter. God is close to us no matter what the season may be.

The Bible teaches us that life is like the seasons. Just as the seasons bring changes in the weather, so there are times of change in each of our lives. There are times we are happy and times we are sad. There are times we are rowdy and times we are calm. There are times we are messy and times we are neat.

But just as God is with us through all the seasons—winter, spring, summer, and fall—God is also with us when we are happy or sad, rowdy or calm, messy or neat. God is always with us.

Dear God, thank you for the different seasons we see as the weather changes. And thank you that you are with us throughout all the changes in our lives. Amen.

Serving One Another

Scripture: Serve one another in love (Gal. 5:13).

Concept: We serve Jesus by helping others.

Object: A glass of water.

Let's think today of ways in which we can serve Jesus. First, let's talk about what it means to serve. When you serve somebody, you work for him. Whatever he needs, you get it for him. When you go to a restaurant, the waitress is there to serve you. She will write down what you want to eat, bring the food to you, and fill up your glass of water as it gets empty. She serves you by doing things for you that you need. When your dad or mom fills up the car with gas, they may go to a self-serve or a full-serve gas station. "Self-serve" means that you work for yourself. "Full-serve" means that someone will work for you, putting gas in your car, checking the air in the tires, and doing whatever is needed.

So, serving Jesus means we work for him. But it may seem difficult to serve Jesus since we can't see him.

But in the Bible Jesus tells us the best way to serve him. He says that we serve him by serving others.

Suppose that a new boy came to our Sunday school class. When he came in, we could tell that he was sad and a little scared because it was his first day. What could we do to help him? *(Pause for response.)* We could talk to him and be friends with him, couldn't we?

Now let's pretend that a girl who was riding her bike in front of your house fell and hurt herself. She couldn't even get up and she was crying. What could you do to help her? *(Pause for response.)* You could get your mom or dad to help her, couldn't you?

Now, let's think about this glass of water I have with me. How might you use a glass of water to help someone? *(Pause for response.)* On a very hot day, water can help. Suppose your dad was working in the yard on a hot day, and you could tell he was getting very thirsty. You could get him a glass of water, couldn't you?

There are many things we can do for people. And as we serve them, we are serving Jesus, too.

Dear God, help us to serve one another in love. Thank you for loving us. Amen.

45

God Never Sleeps

Scripture: He will not let your foot slip—
he who watches over you will not slumber
(Ps. 121:3).

Concept: Since God is always awake, we can
go to him with our problems anytime.

Object: An alarm clock.

What is an alarm clock used for? *(Pause for response.)* Of course, it tells time. Many alarm clocks have radios built in so they can play music. But all alarm clocks also do one other thing. They wake us up.

Do any of you wake up by an alarm clock? *(Pause for response.)* What time do you wake up in the morning? *(Pause for response.)* People wake up at different times. Some people get up very early in order to get to work or school. Others like to sleep in and get up later in the day.

What time do you think God gets up in the morning? *(Pause for response.)* The Bible tells us exactly what time God gets up. It tells us that God never gets up. Do you know why? *(Pause for response.)* God never gets up because God never goes to sleep. God doesn't need to sleep, because he isn't like us. He isn't human. He is God.

It is a good thing that God never sleeps. Since God never sleeps, that means whenever we have a problem, no matter when it is, we can talk to God about it. God doesn't care if it is 2:30 in the morning or 2:30 in the afternoon. He never gets tired and always is happy to hear from us and help us if we are in trouble.

So, although we get tired and need sleep every day, God never gets tired and never sleeps. He is always awake and listening when we need to talk to him.

Dear God, thank you for always being ready to help us, day or night. Amen.

46

Tell the Story

Scripture: It has always been my ambition to preach the gospel (Rom. 15:20).

Concept: We should share the story of Jesus with others.

Object: A storybook.

Some children like to hear a story at night when they go to bed. How many of you like a bedtime story? *(Pause for response.)* Do you have a favorite story? *(Pause for response.)* This is a good story. I've read it many times. Some stories I like to read over and over.

Let's pretend that I was at your house, and you wanted to hear a bedtime story. I told you that I would read the story. So, you went to your books and picked out your favorite story. You gave the book to me to read and got into bed. I sat down in a chair beside the bed, opened the book, and began to read. But instead of reading the book out loud, I read it to myself. Would you enjoy the story if I read it to myself? *(Pause for response.)* No, for you to enjoy the story, I have to tell it to you.

The gospel is the story of Jesus. We find the gospel story in the Bible. It is a story that we can hear over and over and always enjoy. But the story of Jesus isn't a story just to read to ourselves. It is like the bedtime story. We need to tell the story to other people so that they can enjoy it and learn about Jesus.

So, let's enjoy reading the Bible and learning about all the things that Jesus did. But let's also share the story of Jesus with others so that they can enjoy it too.

Thank you, God, for the story about Jesus. Help us to share it with our friends. Amen.

47

Trusting in God's Strength

Scripture: Finally, be strong in the Lord and in his mighty power (Eph. 6:10).

Concept: God is stronger than anyone, so we should trust in him for help.

Objects: Three telephone books.

We need three volunteers today. Which of you would like to help? *(Select three children.)* We need to find the three strongest people in the church. Each of you find one person that you think is the strongest person in the church and bring him or her back here with you. *(Allow the children to begin their search.)*

Okay, we now have the three strongest people in the church. Let's try to find out which of the three is the strongest. To do that, we will give each person a phone book. All our strong people have to do is tear the phone book in half. The person who tears the phone book in half first is the strongest. *(Make sure the adult volunteers understand that the book must remain closed and all pages must be torn simultaneously. Give a book to each adult and let them begin. Allow about thirty seconds to pass.)*

Something is wrong. None of our strong people could tear the phone book in half. Maybe they aren't as strong as we thought they were.

But let me tell you something. Even the strongest person is weak compared to God. That is why it is silly to try to live without God. When we have a problem that is too hard for us to handle by ourselves, God can help us to be stronger. Suppose someone at school is making fun of you. God can help you to be strong when people are unkind. Suppose your family is moving to a new town, and you are afraid of making new friends. God can help you to be strong when you are afraid. We can trust God to give us the strength we need for each day.

Dear God, thank you for giving us the strength we need. Help us to trust in you every day. Amen.

48

God Protects Us

Scripture: For he guards the course of the just and protects the way of his faithful ones (Prov. 2:8).

Concept: God protects us from the devil, even though we can't see him protecting us.

Object: A bottle of sunblock.

I have a bottle of sunblock. Have any of you ever used sunblock? *(Pause for response.)* What does sunblock do? *(Pause for response.)* How do you use sunblock? *(Pause for response.)*

Sunblock protects us from the sun. If we play out in the sun, the sun can burn our skin. When we spread sunblock over our skin, it keeps the sun from giving us a sunburn.

Have any of you ever had a sunburn? *(Pause for response.)* I have, too. Sunburns are not fun. They are painful. The sunblock does a wonderful thing as it protects us from the pain caused by a sunburn.

After you spread the sunblock on your skin, can you see it? *(Pause for response.)* Let's try this sunblock and see how it works. *(Apply a drop of sunblock to the back of your hand or the hand of a volunteer.)* After we spread the sunblock on, we can't see it anymore. It's invisible. But even though we can't see it, it still is working to protect us from the sun.

The Bible says God protects us. In one way, his protection is like the sunblock. The devil would like to make bad things happen to us. He would like to bring pain to our lives. He would like us not to have any joy that comes from Jesus. However, God protects us from the devil. Do we see God protecting us from the devil? *(Pause for response.)* No, we don't see him. But just as the sunblock protects us from the sun even when it is invisible, God protects us from the devil even though we can't see him. It is wonderful that God loves us and protects us.

Dear God, thank you for protecting us. Help us to trust in you even though we can't see you. Amen.

49

Think about Good Things

Scripture: Finally, brothers, whatever is true, whatever is noble, whatever is right, whatever is pure, whatever is lovely, whatever is admirable—if anything is excellent or praiseworthy—think about such things (Phil. 4:8).

Concept: Although there are problems every day, we should think more about the good things.

Object: A new box of crayons. In advance of the lesson, break one of the crayons and put it back in the box with the others.

Look what I have! I have a brand-new box of crayons! I like crayons when they are new. They look so pretty in the box! Let's look at them. *(Open the lid and look at the crayons with the children.)*

What is your favorite color? *(Pause for response. Find the crayons that match the colors mentioned and point to them.)* My favorite color is blue. I like blue because it reminds me of the sky and the ocean. Here is the blue crayon. Let's take it out and look at it. *(Take out the blue crayon that has been previously broken.)*

Oh, no! Something happened to my blue crayon! It's broken! And blue is my favorite. This makes me feel a little sad.

But there's another way to look at this. Although one of my crayons is broken, all the other crayons are in perfect shape! And although my blue crayon is broken, it still can be used. Now that it is broken, two people can color blue at the same time!

This box of crayons is like our lives. When I opened the box I found a beautiful assortment of crayons. I also found one broken crayon. Every day there are many beautiful things God does for us. But there are always a few problems in each day, too.

We can choose to think only of the bad things of life, just as I could have chosen to think only about the broken blue crayon. But that is not good. We need to think also about the many good things of life. So as we talk to God each day, let's not only ask him to help us with our problems, but let's also remember to thank him for the good things he does.

Dear God, thank you for all the good things you do for us each day. You are wonderful, and we love you. Amen.

50

Using Time to Please God

Scripture: Teach us to number our days aright, that we may gain a heart of wisdom (Ps. 90:12).

Concept: Our time is God's time; we should use it to make him happy.

Object: An electric clock (non-digital) with a sweep second hand. Be prepared to plug it into an electrical outlet.

What is a clock good for? *(Pause for response.)* Clocks help us measure time. As we watch the second hand move around the dial of the clock, we can tell how much time is going by.

Sometimes I wish I could slow down time. I have many things to do and not enough time to do them. Watching this clock has given me an idea. I think I know how to make time last longer. *(Unplug the clock.)* Look at the clock now. The second hand is not moving at all. I'll have more time to do things now, won't I? *(Pause for response.)*

Time doesn't work that way at all, does it? I can't slow down time or make it stop just because I unplug the clock. Time keeps on going even when my clock stops.

Who made time? *(Pause for response.)* God made time. The Bible says that God was here before anything else, even time. He made time when he made the world. Since God made time, time belongs to God.

As we live each day, we use the time God has given us. It's really not our time. It's God's time that he lets us use. Since it is God's time, we should use it in ways that please him. What are some things we can do to please God? *(Pause for response.)* Yes, there are many things we can do that make God happy. Let's spend the time God gives us in doing things that please him.

Dear God, thank you for every day we live. Help us to use the time you give us in ways that please you. Amen.